Facing Mighty Fears
About Animals

Dr. Dawn's Mini Books About Mighty Fears
By Dawn Huebner, PhD
Illustrated by Liza Stevens
Helping children ages 6–10 live happier lives

Facing Mighty Fears About Health
ISBN 978 1 78775 928 2
eISBN 978 1 78775 927 5

Facing Mighty Fears About Throwing Up
ISBN 978 1 78775 925 1
eISBN 978 1 78775 926 8

Facing Mighty Fears About Trying New Things
ISBN 978 1 78775 950 3
eISBN 978 1 78775 951 0

Watch for future titles in the
Dr. Dawn's Mini Books About Mighty Fears series.

Facing Mighty Fears About Animals

Dawn Huebner, PhD

Illustrated by Liza Stevens

Jessica Kingsley Publishers
London and Philadelphia

First published in Great Britain in 2022 by Jessica Kingsley Publishers
An imprint of Hodder & Stoughton Ltd
An Hachette Company

1

A CIP catalogue record for this title is available from the
British Library and the Library of Congress

ISBN 978 1 78775 946 6
eISBN 978 1 78775 947 3

Printed and bound in Great Britain by TJ Books Limited

Jessica Kingsley Publishers' policy is to use papers that are natural,
renewable, and recyclable products and made from wood grown in
sustainable forests. The logging and manufacturing processes are expected
to conform to the environmental regulations of the country of origin.

Jessica Kingsley Publishers
Carmelite House
50 Victoria Embankment
London EC4Y 0DZ

www.jkp.com

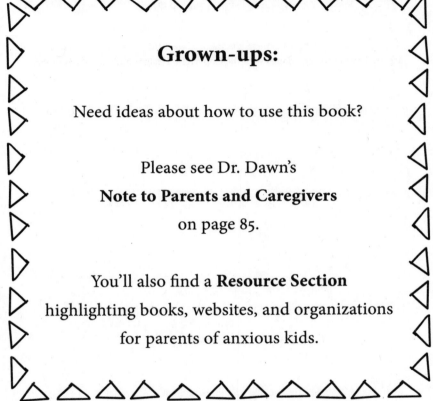

Grown-ups:

Need ideas about how to use this book?

Please see Dr. Dawn's
Note to Parents and Caregivers
on page 85.

You'll also find a **Resource Section**
highlighting books, websites, and organizations
for parents of anxious kids.

There are animals that:

CRAWL

Pounce

Slither

RUN

Creep

CLIMB

BITE

STING

Jump

Leap

PLAY

Swim

FIGHT

Dig

GROOM

FLY

Dive

Stalk

H o p

Hide

There are animals that choose to be with humans…

…and animals that scurry away
when humans come near.

There are animals that are helpful to humans…

FUN FACT
Dogs can be trained to
smell signs of cancer,
diabetes, and epilepsy
in the humans who
own them.

FUN FACT
It takes 12 worker bees
to produce one teaspoon
of honey. Some of that is
used by the hive. Humans
get to eat the rest.

FUN FACT
Scientists can "milk"
snakes to get their
venom, which can be
used as medicine.

…and animals we do best to avoid.

Why do we avoid certain animals?

Well, some animals smell bad.

FUN FACT
Some bugs fart, but
the gas comes out in
such small quantities
that we don't smell it.

Some look creepy, slimy, freaky, or weird.

FUN FACT
Bees have five eyes, six legs, and short, thick bodies covered with hair. Yup, hair!

FUN FACT
Spiders have short hairs on their feet that allow them to walk upside down on ceilings.

FUN FACT
Spider legs are oily, so they don't get stuck in their own webs.

Some animals are loud, which is startling.

Or silent, so they take us by surprise.

FUN FACT
Snakes don't have regular
ears, so they "hear" with their
jaws. The bones in a snake's
lower jaw pick up vibrations in
the ground, which is how they
know when something is near.

But mostly, we avoid animals that are dangerous: animals that **ATTACK**,

or **BITE**,

or otherwise **HURT** humans.

If you avoid animals that most people avoid—like sharks, for example, or scorpions—that's okay. Some animals really are **DANGEROUS**.

If you avoid animals that don't live near you, that's not a problem either. You are never going to encounter them, so it doesn't really matter.

It's different, though, if you avoid animals that live near you, animals that other people are able to be around (like bees) or even enjoy (like dogs).

FUN FACT
Bees have a long tube similar to a trunk called the proboscis, which helps them take in nectar from flowers.

FUN FACT
Bees collect pollen by putting it into "pockets" built right into their legs.

FUN FACT
When the weather is warm, thousands of worker bees use their wings to fan the hive, helping the queen, larvae (baby bees), and honey stay cool. When it is cold, worker bees surround the queen, shed their wings, and shiver, producing heat to keep her comfy and warm.

If you feel as if you have to avoid common animals, life can get pretty complicated.

It's exhausting to always be on the lookout for the kind of animal you avoid.

You may have to make decisions about where to go or not go depending on whether the animal is likely to be there.

If you are reading this book, chances are good that you avoid a common animal, an animal other people are okay being around.

Usually, that kind of avoidance is based on **FEAR**.

FUN FACT
Fear of dogs is called cynophobia.
Fear of bees is called melissophobia.
Fear of spiders is called arachnophobia.
Fear of snakes is called ophidiophobia.
Fear of cats is called ailurophobia.
Fear of cows is called bovinophobia.
Fear of toads is called bufonophobia.
Fear of horses is called equinophobia.

What kind of animal do you avoid?

Has avoiding that animal made it hard to go places or do things?

Have you noticed that not everyone shares your fear?

It's curious how that works, isn't it?

It seems so obvious to you that the kind of animal you avoid needs to be avoided, but other people don't see it that way.

Why is that?

Well, we all have an internal alarm system tucked deep within our brain.

Most of the time, this brain alarm works exactly as it should, alerting us to actual danger.

But every once in a while, it makes a mistake. This is called a false alarm.

False alarms are when our brain tells us we need to avoid something that is actually quite safe.

FUN FACT
Not all bees and wasps sting people. Male bees don't even have stingers!

FUN FACT
Spiders do not feed on human blood. They never chase people, and only bite when they feel threatened.

Why do false alarms happen?

False alarms happen for lots of reasons.

We see something, or hear about something, or imagine something—something that may not be true, or that is true but quite unusual—and our brain tells us:

Maybe the kind of animal you are afraid of once scared you.

Maybe it hurt you.

FUN FACT
There are approximately 900 million dogs in the world.

FUN FACT
Dogs yawn to calm themselves when they are scared.

FUN FACT
Just like we have unique fingerprints, dogs have unique nose prints.

Maybe you heard about someone having trouble with that kind of animal, or you saw a movie or read a book about it.

Whatever set it off to begin with, your brain now tells you that being around that kind of animal is **DANGEROUS**. Always.

And you need to stay away from it. Always.

But if what happened was a one-time thing, or if what you heard or imagined isn't true, then this is a false alarm.

There is no real danger.

FUN FACT
Dogs wag their tails to the left when they are scared. They wag low when they feel nervous or unsure.

FUN FACT
Snakes can't bite into food so they only eat what they can swallow whole.

False alarms are a problem because you end up avoiding something that is scary but safe. But your brain thinks:

Whew! It's a good thing I avoided that thing.

And then you get caught in this loop of fear →
avoidance → relief → fear → avoidance → relief →
fear → avoidance → relief. All about something that
scared you but is not actually dangerous.

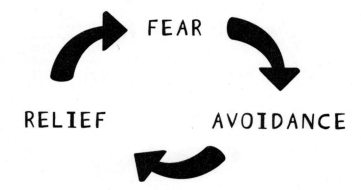

When you get stuck in the fear → avoidance → relief
loop, you are teaching your brain that staying away
is the right thing—the **only** thing—to do.

But if you feel **SCARED**, what else (besides staying away) can you do?

FUN FACT
Dogs have an excellent sense of smell, about one million times stronger than that of humans.

FUN FACT
Dogs have 18 different muscles they use to move their ears. They can hear sounds four times further away than humans.

FUN FACT
Dogs were sent into outer space before humans. The first dog in space was a Russian Siberian husky named Laika.

Well, if you had a magic wand—then, presto!—you could make spiders, or bees, or whatever kind of animal you are afraid of disappear.

But magic wands are in short supply, and if you had one, you might want to use it for something better than making pesky animals disappear.

Fortunately, there's another way to help yourself—a way that doesn't rely on wands. And the good news is, you already know how to do it.

The technique is called **exposure**, and it works well to shrink even stubborn (big, long-lasting) fears.

To understand exposure, picture this:

It's a warm day, and you are going swimming with a friend.

You walk to the edge of the pool, and jump in.

Brrrrrrrrr!

Pool water feels cold when you first jump in.

But there you are, in that cold water. So, what do you do?

Well, if you're like most kids, you probably start swimming or playing.

And then, after a while, the water starts to feel better.

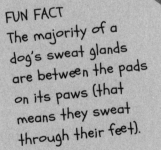

FUN FACT
The majority of a dog's sweat glands are between the pads on its paws (that means they sweat through their feet).

FUN FACT
Snakes need the heat of the sun to stay warm.

Why is that?

Has the water warmed up?

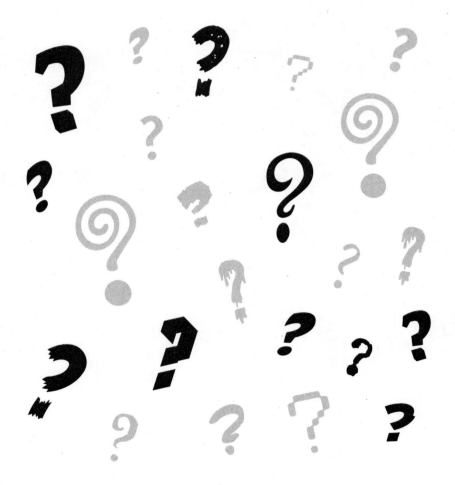

Nope.

The temperature of the water hasn't changed.

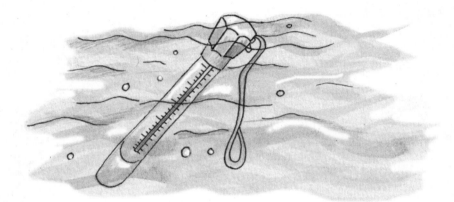

You have.

You expose yourself to the water.

It feels cold.

But you stay in the pool, and over time, your brain and your body adjust.

You get used to it.

It's funny how that works. Almost like magic.
Except there is no magic.

Your brain and your body just know what to do.

FUN FACT
Snake scales are smooth and fit
together perfectly so there is no
place for dirt to get caught. Even
snakes that slither around in
dirt all day never have to bathe.

FUN FACT
Snakes don't have eyelids. Their
eyes are protected by a special
clear scale that gets shed along
with the rest of their skin.

In fact, you do this all the time:

→ You get used to the water in a shower or bath.

→ You get used to strong smells in a restaurant.

→ You get used to the volume of a movie.

→ You get used to the sound of construction trucks in your neighborhood.

→ You get used to shoes that feel funny on your feet.

The longer you keep yourself in these situations—
these **uncomfortable** situations—the more your
brain and your body adjust.

FUN FACT
Insects don't have the right
kind of glands to make
tears, so they can't cry.

FUN FACT
As sweat and bacteria
build up, dog paws
start to smell like corn
chips. This is sometimes
called "Frito feet."

Okay, okay—there was an important word in that last sentence: uncomfortable.

You might be thinking, "What's going on with animals is totally different."

I'm not uncomfortable. I'm SCARED.

Fair enough.

You are scared.

But the truth is, you are safe.

Your fear is a scary, **uncomfortable** false alarm, so exposure is still the way to go.

FUN FACT
Some snakes play dead when they are afraid. They flip onto their backs, open their mouths, and stick out their tongues, hoping to trick their prey.

FUN FACT
Snakes are helpful to humans. Small ones eat harmful bugs; large ones eat rats and mice.

FUN FACT
If left alone, spiders will eat most of the pesky insects in a house: mosquitos, moths, earwigs, flies, and roaches. They even eat each other!

We can get used to scary-but-safe animals the same way we get used to cold water, loud noises, and smelly smells.

We can **expose** ourselves to them and we'll get used to them.

FUN FACT
Dogs lick their lips when they are nervous. They also lick their lips after delicious meals.

FUN FACT
Each dog has a unique smell that comes from glands near its rear end. That's why dogs sniff one another's bottoms, so they can get to know each other.

That might sound hard, but you get to be in charge of how to do this.

Think about the swimming pool again.

You have a choice about how to get in, right?

You can jump in, or you can go step by step.

It's the same with fears.

You can "jump in" all at once to get used to whatever you are afraid of, or you can go step by step.

Taking it step by step is slower, which makes it easier. It's the way most kids choose to tackle their animal fears.

And there's another thing. What you are learning will work with **any** scary-but-safe animal, or bug, or slithery thing.

We've been talking about the most common animal fears—dogs, spiders, bees, and snakes— but those are just examples. The specific animal doesn't matter.

It's the technique—the exposure—that's
the important part.

So, just plug in the kind of animal you fear,
whatever that is, and follow the three steps you are
about to learn, which spell out the word: win.

Step One: **W**illing

Step Two: **I**nterested

Step Three: **N**ear

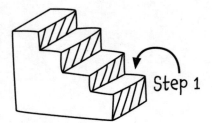

Step 1

Step 1. willing

For a technique to work, you have to be **willing** to do it.

Willing, as you know, is different from eager or happy.

It's when you know something is going to be hard, but you decide to do it anyway.

Most people are willing to do things that matter to them, or things that bring some sort of reward.

You jump into a cold pool (the hard part) because you know that swimming is fun (the reward).

You **want** to swim, so you are **willing** to put up with the initial shock of cold water.

FUN FACT
Wasps have a sweet tooth, just like many humans. They make a point of finding the sweetest plants and fruits, as well as the tastiest insects.

FUN FACT
Bees visit up to 100 flowers in a single collection trip.

FUN FACT
Honeybees beat their wings 200 times per second.

Or you might be **willing** to wear a sports uniform that isn't as comfortable as your regular clothes, because you **want** to be on the team.

Once you decide that you are willing to do something, it gets easier.

So, before you move on to the next step, think about what makes you **willing** to face your fear of animals.

What do you **want** to be able to do?

Here's what some kids say:

I want to go to
birthday parties
without worrying
about dogs.

I want to
go to the
beach.

I want to
get a pet.

I want to play in
the garden without
always looking out
for bees.

I want to fall
asleep without
worrying about
spiders.

I want to
get a puppy.

Pause for a moment to find a piece of paper.

Then, think about what you want to be able to do, and how you will feel once you are able to do that thing.

Write down what you want, and how you will feel.

want - to go to
my friend's house
feel - happy and
proud

Remembering why you are doing this will help you be more **willing** to work on your fear.

When you are done writing, put the paper someplace easy to see. Maybe on your nightstand. Or in the kitchen.

Next time the steps you are taking feel scary and uncomfortable, when you start to think, "This is too hard!", look at your paper.

Knowing that your life will get easier—that things will be better—can help you to stay motivated and strong.

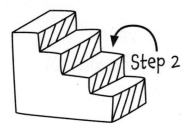

Step 2. Interested

No matter what animal you are afraid of, there are people who love that kind of animal.

People who study it or work to protect it.

People who like thinking and talking about it.

People who go looking for that animal—
on purpose!

People who choose to be around it.

Why is that?

Why do some people like the animal you try your hardest to avoid?

FUN FACT

> Entomologists study bugs.

> Melittologists study bees.

> Herpetologists study snakes (and other reptiles and amphibians).

> Arachnologists study spiders (and mites, ticks, and scorpions).

> Cynologists study dogs. Veterinarians do, too.

Well, for one thing, animals are interesting. Also, many of them are helpful to us and our planet.

All animals have something going for them.

Chances are good that you don't know a whole lot about the animal you fear other than the fact that it seems scary. But there's something important you need to know:

We often fear things we don't understand.

Fortunately, there's something you can do about that because facts reduce fears.

So, with this second step, you'll be learning facts about the animal you fear.

Go online, or go to the library, or ask a grown-up to help you find out:

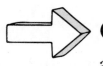 **Question #1**: What are your animal's habits?

 Question #2: Why do they look the way they look?

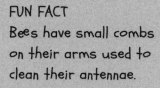

FUN FACT
Bees have small combs on their arms used to clean their antennae.

FUN FACT
Snakes smell with their tongues. That's why they flick them.

Question #3: What does it mean when your animal barks, or pants, or buzzes?

 Question #4: How does your animal communicate?

 Question #5: What does your animal eat?

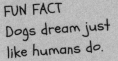

FUN FACT
Dogs dream just like humans do.

FUN FACT
Spiders don't eat their prey, they drink them! Spider mouths are so small that they need to turn the insects they catch into liquid so they can suck them up.

FUN FACT
Spiders eat insects, but they can't taste with their mouths. The hairs on a spider's front legs are sensitive to taste, so they "taste" with their feet!

FUN FACT
Dogs wag their tails
to the right when
they are happy.
Wagging in circles (like
a helicopter) means
they are super happy.

FUN FACT
When they have found a
tasty food source, worker
bees return to the hive
and do a patterned "waggle
dance" to let other bees
know how to find the food.

FUN FACT
Honeybees have a special gland that
allows them to make "royal jelly." All
larvae (baby bees) get fed a bit of this
jelly, but one larva is given a constant
diet of it, which turns her into a queen.

Question #6: What are the young of your animal called?

FUN FACT

Baby spiders are called spiderlings.

Baby ants are called antlings.

Baby bats are called pups.

Baby bees are called larvae.

Baby coyotes are called whelps.

Baby foxes are called kits.

Baby goats are called kids.

Baby hedgehogs are called hoglets.

Baby kangaroos are called joeys.

Baby mosquitos are called wrigglers.

Baby pigeons are called squeakers.

Baby platypus are called puggles.

Baby porcupines are called porcupettes.

Baby skunks are called kittens.

Baby snakes are called snakelets.

Question #7: How do the grown-ups care for their young?

FUN FACT

Spiderlings use silk to travel through the air. This is called ballooning because the wind catches the silk and helps the little spider drift around.

FUN FACT

Wolf spiders lay their eggs on a pad of silk which they turn into a ball and attach near their tail. When the eggs hatch, the little spiders crawl onto their mother's back, where they ride for days or even weeks.

FUN FACT
Puppies eyes are sealed when they are born. It takes two weeks for them to start to see.

FUN FACT
Snakes outgrow their skin. Every few months, they rub against the ground or branches to help them slither—inside-out, like a sock—from their too-tight skin. But snakes are never naked because there's always a new, right-size skin underneath.

FUN FACT
Spiders that create webs spin a new one every day. What happens to all those day-old webs? Well, spiders are good about cleaning up after themselves. Some spiders eat their old webs. Others roll them up and throw them away.

Question #8: What do people like or find interesting about your animal?

So, type "fun facts" about your animal into a search engine.

No matter what kind of animal you put in, you'll see lots of interesting, funny, useful, bizarre things—facts like the ones you've seen throughout this book.

Let the facts begin to calm your fears.

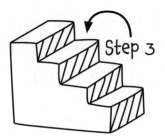

Step 3. Near

Now it's time to start exposing yourself directly to the kind of animal you fear. It's time to get closer.

The goal is to let your brain and body begin to get used to the animal, and to the discomfort you feel when you are near it.

This is the "getting into the water" step, and just like the swimming pool, it's okay to go slowly.

Work with your parents to come up with a list of activities involving your animal.

Think especially about the things you've been avoiding, like going certain places or doing certain things.

Think about how to break the scariest-seeming activities into small steps.

Be creative.

Make at least some of your activities interesting and fun. Feel free to include art, or photography, or made-up games.

Some of the activities you and your parents talk about might seem too hard, but that's okay. You won't be doing everything at once.

To get you started, look at the examples in this book, including the sample lists on the next few pages.

Copy down the activities you like, then come up with more of your own.

Remember, you can exchange one animal for another, so look at all of the lists and think about how you might change activities to fit the kind of animal you are trying to get used to.

Sample list: Dogs

Watch a dog from inside your car

Stand out of reach of a dog on a leash

Let a dog on a leash sniff your hand

Toss a ball for a dog to run after

Stand near a barking dog on a leash

Watch someone comb their dog

Feed a dog a treat

Shake hands with a dog that knows how to shake

Stand near a sleeping dog

Walk past a dog on a leash

Watch several dogs playing from far away

Go to a place where you are likely to see lots of dogs (like a dog park) and do a scavenger hunt, trying to find a dog with a fancy collar, a dog taller than your knees, a tiny dog, a dog with droopy ears, a dog that is drooling, a barking dog, and so on

Make a card to play dog BINGO with a different breed of dog in each square. Put an X on the square when you see that kind of dog

Sample list: Bees

Look at a bee in a jar (your parent can capture one for you, then let it go when you are done)

Hold a jar that has a bee in it

Go outside on a day when there might be bees

Go on a bee scavenger hunt, trying to spot a bee near a pink flower, near a white one, near a garbage pail, a bee that is flying, a bee that has landed on something, and so on

Go to a place where you've seen bees before

Walk to a different part of your yard when you see a bee (but still stay outside)

Go on a bee photo safari, taking pictures of the bees you see

Move a few steps away when you see a bee, but close enough to still see it

Look at a dead bee someone else is holding

Hold a dead bee

Watch an active hive online

Sample list: Spiders

Look at a spider in a covered jar

Hold a covered jar containing a spider

Hold an open jar containing a spider

Let a spider climb onto a large piece of paper, then bring the paper outside to set it free

Go into your basement or garage to count spiders. See who can find three spiders first

Stay in a room that has a spider in it

Sit near a spider to draw it

Find out what kinds of spiders live in your area. Make a spider BINGO card and put an X on the square of each kind of spider as you see it

Stand near a spider on the wall

Stand under a spider on the ceiling

Look at a spider's web up close. Try to draw it

Go outside early in the morning and try to find a web that still has dew on it. Try to find a web with a dead insect in it, and then a web with a spider on it

Take a close-up picture of a spider

Watch a spider as it moves across a wall or the ceiling; see if you can predict where it will go

Sample list: Non-poisonous snakes

Look at non-poisonous snakes online

Find out which kinds of snakes live near you, make a BINGO card of those snakes and put an x on the square as you see them

Go on walks in places where there are likely to be non-poisonous snakes

Go on a snake photo safari, trying to find snakes to take pictures of

Find someone with a pet snake (or go to a pet store or zoo) to look at snakes in cages

Stand near a caged snake long enough to draw it

Stand across the room from someone holding a snake

Stand near someone holding a snake

Touch a snake that someone else is holding

After you have listed a bunch of activities, sort your list into three categories: easy, medium, and hard.

You'll know which category to put each activity into by paying attention to how scared it makes you feel when you think about doing it.

The goal is to come up with at least five activities in each category (easy, medium, and hard).

If none seem easy, think about ways to modify some of the "mediums" to make them easier, like standing further away, or having a parent right by your side.

Once you have sorted your list, start doing the activities in the easy group. These should be things you can accomplish with just a little extra bravery. Not things you are already doing, but things you can push yourself to do.

Don't wait until you happen to encounter your animal; go looking for it.

Exposure is something you do on purpose.

Set aside time to practice every day—multiple times a day would be even better.

Do all of the activities in the easy group, then do them again. Perhaps several times. Then move on to the activities in the medium group, and so on.

Let's say you have moved through all the activities in the easy category, and the medium category, and now you are on the hard category.

Pretend one of your hard activities is to hold an open jar with a spider inside. Your parent finds the spider and  scoops it into the jar. You reach for the jar...and find you totally can't do it. It feels TOO HARD.

DON'T PANiC.

This is just like moving from waist-deep to chest-deep water in a pool.

If the water feels TOO COLD, you're not going to get out of the pool entirely, are you? Of course not. You're just going to take a single step back.

It's the same with getting closer to the animal you fear.

If you start to do a step and it feels too hard, don't give up. Just figure out a way to make the step a little easier. Loosely cover the jar, for example. Or keep it open but don't hold it.

Do the easier step repeatedly. Pretty soon, you'll be able to do more.

So, that's it.

You know what you need to know to WIN against your fear. Just follow the three steps:

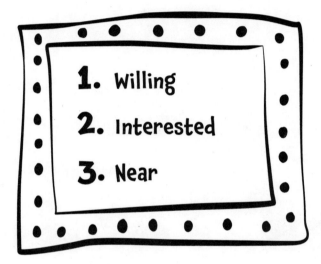

1. Willing
2. Interested
3. Near

Re-read this book if you need to. Focus on the steps one at a time. Practice. Practice. Practice.

Remind yourself that your fear is a false alarm, and that you have the power to help your brain and your body adjust.

You can do it!

And then you can get on with your life.

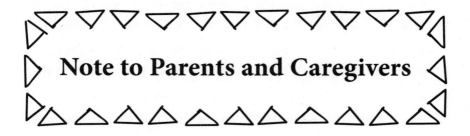

Note to Parents and Caregivers

Animal fears are among the most common fears experienced by school-age children. If you have picked up this book, however, the chances are good that the fear your child is exhibiting has gone beyond what seems "normal" to you. You see your child panicking, needing ever more reassurance to do basic things. You find yourself scanning for bees, for spiders, for dogs, hoping against hope that you'll be able to get through this outing, this playdate, this bedtime without incident. Avoiding the animal your child fears has become a way of life. No one wants to live that way. No one wants that for their child.

What can you do? You have surely seen that reassurance does nothing to reduce fears like this (called phobias), fears grossly out of proportion to the actual danger. In fact, reassurance becomes counterproductive, especially when coupled with fostering your child's avoidance. A phobic child is responding to an internal misperception. A danger alarm gone awry. The only way to correct this is to guide your child through repeated practice being around the animal they fear—in measured doses, increasing over time. This is called *exposure*: systematic, frequent, intentional practice being around dogs, or spiders, or whatever it is that your child fears.

This book walks you and your child through exposure—what it is, why it works, and how to do it. Your child will benefit most if you read the book together. Pause to talk about the content, helping your child think about how it applies to them, and how they might use it. Linger over the fun facts scattered throughout this book. Reading about the animal your child fears is itself a form of exposure.

Move away from avoidance by seeking out the animal your child fears. Find pictures to use as screen savers. Place quirky and interesting representations of the animal—books, cartoons, stuffed animals—around your house. When you see it out in the world, imagine a life for the animal, perhaps use a funny voice to speak for it. Your child needs direct experience thinking about, talking about, and—importantly—being around the feared animal. That's the only way they will begin to recognize that the animal is scary but safe—and then, over time, not so scary.

Some additional tips

1. Not all dogs are friendly. Some stinging insects really are aggressive. Some spiders do need to be avoided. Take the time to learn about the kind of animal your child fears. Then, as you make your way through this book, make distinctions between, for example, honeybees and yellow jackets, or a barking rottweiler and your neighbor's chocolate lab. Help your child learn to make these distinctions too.

2. Teach your child how to safely interact with unknown animals.

Caution makes sense. But caution is different from paralyzing fear. Paralyzing fear is the target of this book.

3. Be aware of your own level of anxiety. If your child's panic makes your own anxiety skyrocket, you may need additional support. There's no shame in that. Please seek the help you need.

4. If anxiety is significantly interfering with your child's life or the life of your family, please reach out to a mental health professional able to guide you in the use of exposure and other tools.

5. As you are reading this book, remain warm and empathic. Encourage your child to take brave steps, saying things like, "I know this feels scary" and, "I know you can do it." Keep your breathing steady. Your calm sends a message to the primitive part of your child's brain that is always on the lookout for danger. Make sure you are signaling safety and confidence in your child.

6. Help your child implement the three steps outlined in this book. They are the key to breaking free from oversized fears.

You can do this. Your child can do this. I'll be rooting for you.

Dr. Dawn

Resources

Organizations

These organizations provide information about childhood anxiety, and include therapist locators to assist with finding specialized care:

USA

The Anxiety and Depression Association of America:
https://adaa.org

The International OCD Foundation:
https://iocdf.org

UK

Anxiety UK:
www.anxietyuk.org.uk

Young Minds:
https://youngminds.org.uk

AU/NZ

Beyond Blue:
www.beyondblue.org.au

Kids Health:
https://kidshealth.org.nz

Please also reach out to your child's pediatrician for names of local providers.

Web-based resources

https://library.jkp.com
Dr. Dawn's Seven-Step Solution for When Worry Takes Over: Easy-to-Implement Strategies for Parents or Carers of Anxious Kids, see page 94.
Video Training Course

www.anxioustoddlers.com
Natasha Daniels of AT Parenting Survival creates podcasts, blog posts, and free resources about anxiety. She also offers subscription courses, coaching, and treatment.

https://childmind.org
This NY Institute offers articles on a host of topics, including anxiety, with a unique "Ask an Expert" feature providing trustworthy, relatable advice.

https://copingskillsforkids.com
Janine Halloran provides free, easy-to-implement, child-friendly tips on calming anxiety, managing stress, and more.

https://gozen.com
Kid-tested, therapist-approved, highly effective animated videos teaching skills related to anxiety, resilience, emotional intelligence, and more.

www.worrywisekids.org
Tamar Chansky of WorryWiseKids provides a treasure-trove of information for parents of anxious children.

Recommended reading

There are many appealing, effective books to help children manage worries and fears. Please check with your preferred bookseller, who can guide you towards books particularly suited to your child's needs. Here are a few suggestions.

For younger children

What to Do When You Worry Too Much: A Kid's Guide to Overcoming Anxiety by Dawn Huebner, PhD, American Psychological Association.

Binnie the Baboon Anxiety and Stress Activity Book by Dr. Karen Treisman, Jessica Kingsley Publishers.

Hey Warrior: A Book for Kids about Anxiety by Karen Young, Little Steps Publishing.

Little Meerkat's Big Panic: A Story About Learning New Ways to Feel Calm by Jane Evans, Jessica Kingsley Publishers.

The Nervous Knight: A Story About Overcoming Worries and Anxiety by Anthony Lloyd Jones, Jessica Kingsley Publishers.

Starving the Anxiety Gremlin for Children Aged 5–9: A CBT Workbook on Anxiety Management by Kate Collins-Donnelly, Jessica Kingsley Publishers.

For older children

Outsmarting Worry: An Older Kid's Guide to Managing Anxiety by Dawn Huebner, PhD, Jessica Kingsley Publishers.

All Birds Have Anxiety by Kathy Hoopmann, Jessica Kingsley Publishers.

The Can-Do Kid's Journal: Discover Your Confidence Superpower! by Sue Atkins, Jessica Kingsley Publishers.

Can I Tell You About Anxiety? A Guide for Friends and Family by Lucy Willetts, Jessica Kingsley Publishers.

Doodle Your Worries Away: A CBT Doodling Workbook for Kids Who Feel Worried or Anxious by Tanja Sharpe, Jessica Kingsley Publishers.

Help! I've Got an Alarm Bell Going Off in My Head! How Panic, Anxiety and Stress Affect Your Body by K.L. Aspden, Jessica Kingsley Publishers.

The Panicosaurus: Managing Anxiety in Children, Including those with Asperger Syndrome by K.L. Al-Ghani, Jessica Kingsley Publishers.

Starving the Anxiety Gremlin: A CBT Workbook on Anxiety Management for Young People Aged 10+ by Kate Collins-Donnelly, Jessica Kingsley Publishers.

For parents

Anxious Kids, Anxious Parents by Dr. Reid Wilson and Lynn Lyons, Health Communications Inc.

The A–Z of Therapeutic Parenting: Strategies and Solutions by Sarah Naish, Jessica Kingsley Publishers.

The No Worries Guide to Raising Your Anxious Child by Karen Lynn Cassiday, Jessica Kingsley Publishers.

Parenting Your Anxious Toddler by Natasha Daniels, Jessica Kingsley Publishers.

Peaceful Parent, Happy Kids by Dr. Laura Markham, TarcherPerigee.

The Yes Brain: How to Cultivate Courage, Curiosity and Resilience in Your Child by Dr. Dan Siegel and Dr. Tina Payne Bryson, Bantam Press.

Dr. Dawn's

SEVEN-STEP SOLUTION FOR WHEN WORRY TAKES OVER

Easy-to-Implement Strategies for Parents or Carers of Anxious Kids

worry has a way of turning into WORRY in the blink of an eye. This upper-case WORRY causes children to fret about unlikely scenarios and shrink away from routine challenges, ultimately holding entire families hostage. But upper-case WORRY is predictable and manageable once you understand its tricks.

This 7-video series will help you recognize WORRY's tricks while teaching a handful of techniques to help you and your child break free.

Each video contains learning objectives and action steps along with need-to-know content presented in a clear, engaging manner by child psychologist and best-selling author, Dr. Dawn Huebner. The videos are available from https://library.jkp.com.

Video One: Trolling for Danger (time 8:15)

- The role of the amygdala in spotting and alerting us to danger
- What happens when the amygdala sets off an alarm
- Real dangers versus false alarms
- Calming the brain (yours and your child's) to get back to thinking

Video Two: The Worry Loop (time 10:15)

- The "loop" that keeps Worry in place
- How to identify where your child is in the Worry Loop

Video Three: Externalizing Anxiety (time 11:41)

- Externalizing anxiety as a powerful first step
- Talking back to Worry
- Teaching your child to talk back to Worry
- Talking back without entering into a debate

Video Four: Calming the Brain and Body (time 13:36)

- Breathing techniques
- Mindfulness techniques
- Distraction techniques
- Which technique (how to choose)?

Video Five: Getting Rid of Safety Behaviors (time 15:18)

- Preparation
- The role of exposure
- Explaining exposure to your child
- Creating an exposure hierarchy

Video Six: Worrying Less Is Not the Goal (time 13:02)

- The more you fight anxiety, the more it holds on
- The more you accommodate anxiety, the more it stays
- Anxiety is an error message, a false alarm
- When you stop letting Worry be in charge, it fades

Video Seven: Putting It All Together (time 19:42)

- A review of the main techniques
- Deciding where to start
- The role of rewards
- Supporting your child, not Worry